PTSD RECOVERY

A Step by Step Guide to Survive From Ptsd

(A Beginner's Guide to Ptsd, Causes, Treatment and Recovery)

Fatima Bunting

Published by Tomas Edwards

© **Fatima Bunting**

All Rights Reserved

Ptsd Recovery: A Step by Step Guide to Survive From Ptsd (A Beginner's Guide to Ptsd, Causes, Treatment and Recovery)

ISBN 978-1-990268-56-4

All rights reserved. No part of this guide may be reproduced in any form without permission in writing from the publisher except in the case of brief quotations embodied in critical articles or reviews.

Legal & Disclaimer

The information contained in this book is not designed to replace or take the place of any form of medicine or professional medical advice. The information in this book has been provided for educational and entertainment purposes only.

The information contained in this book has been compiled from sources deemed reliable, and it is accurate to the best of the Author's knowledge; however, the Author cannot guarantee its accuracy and validity and cannot be held liable for any errors or omissions. Changes are periodically made to this book. You must consult your doctor or get professional medical advice before using any of the suggested remedies, techniques, or information in this book.

Upon using the information contained in this book, you agree to hold harmless the Author from and against any damages, costs, and expenses, including any legal fees potentially resulting from the application of any of the information provided by this guide. This disclaimer applies to any damages or injury caused by the use and application, whether directly or indirectly, of any advice or information presented, whether for breach of contract, tort, negligence, personal injury, criminal intent, or under any other cause of action.

You agree to accept all risks of using the information presented inside this book. You need to consult a professional medical practitioner in order to ensure you are both able and healthy enough to participate in this program.

Table of Contents

INTRODUCTION 1

CHAPTER1: PTSD: THE BASICS 4

CHAPTER 2: THE 7 REASONS YOU STILL HAVE PTSD SYMPTOMS 10

CHAPTER 3: HOW PTSD OCCURS & DIAGNOSING IT 17

CHAPTER 4:PREVENTING PTSD AFTER TRAUMA 23

CHAPTER 5: MOVE MOUNTAINS: HEALING POWERS OF MOVEMENT TO COPE WITH PTSD 29

CHAPTER 6: DIAGNOSING PTSD 39

CHAPTER 7: TRUE STORIES OF SPIRITUAL ENCOUNTERS .. 44

CHAPTER 8: CONDITIONING OF YOURSELF 55

CHAPTER 9: SYMPTOMS OF PTSD IN CHILDREN 59

CHAPTER 10: EXPLOSIVE ANGER 80

CHAPTER 11: MENTAL DISORDERS ASSOCIATED WITH PTSD 95

CHAPTER 12: DEALING WITH CATEGORY D SYMPTOMS 103

CHAPTER 13: THE FOUR F'S: FIGHT, FLIGHT, FREEZE AND FAWN 110

CHAPTER 14: SUPPORT 116

CHAPTER 15: MANAGE YOUR TIME 121

CONCLUSION 130

Introduction

Post-traumatic stress disorder (PTSD) is a disorder that is present in some individuals who have had a shocking, frightening or dangerous incident. In and after a traumatic situation, it is natural to feel fear. Fear causes several second-split changes in the body, which help protect or avoid threat. This answer of "fight or flight" is a typical reaction to protect the person against damage. Almost everybody has a range of reactions after trauma, but most people naturally recover from initial symptoms. PTSD can be treated with those who tend to suffer from problems. Persons with PTSD may feel stressed or scared, even if they are not at risk

While there have been a great number of cases in recent years of apparent post-traumatic stress disorder (PTSD), the Diagnostic and Statistical Manual on Mental Illness officially classified PTSD as a psychiatric condition. In subsequent editions, PTSD criteria have been refined and were first included into the 10th edition of the ICD. Box 1 presents its characteristic features. A person must be exposed to traumatic events involving a real or threatened death, serious injury or threat to the physical integrity of themselves or others in order to satisfy the criteria of DSMIV. It is also necessary for each person to experience a response at the time that involves extreme fear, impotence or terror. Symptoms have to be present in a clinically significant social, occupational or other important operations area for a period of at least 1 month (1 month is not classified in the ICD10 range). Acute stress disorder (ASD), with more emphasis on disassociation, occurs within 1 month following a traumatic event with similar symptom criteria to PTSD. If it continues beyond 3 months, Acute PTSD becomes chronic. Symptoms usually start shortly after the trauma but will be delayed if they start at least 6 months later.

Chapter 1: Ptsd: The Basics

Years of war in Iraq and Afghanistan have brought to attention Post Traumatic Stress Disorder (or simply PTSD) like never before. Post Traumatic Stress Disorder is a general term used to describe a psychiatric disorder occurring after you experience or witness an event that puts your life at risk like serious accidents, natural disasters, military combat, terrorist incidents, or even sexual physical assault in adulthood or childhood. Most survivors usually return to normal after some time. However, some people tend to experience stress reactions after the incident that are persistent, or even get worse over time. This is usually the first sign of post-traumatic stress disorder. If you suffer from PTSD, you may relive the experience through flashbacks and nightmares, feel detached or estranged, and have difficulty sleeping. If you fail to address these symptoms, they can become severe and long lasting enough to significantly impair your daily life.

There are basically three sets of symptoms that people with PTSD experience.

*The first group involves reliving the trauma in various ways like getting upset when confronted by a reminder of the trauma, or thinking about the trauma when you are doing something else.

*The second set normally involves either feeling numb or distancing yourself from people or places that remind you of the trauma, and isolating yourself.

*The third set includes such symptoms as startling easily, or feeling irritable and on guard.

Post Traumatic Stress Disorder is marked by clear psychological symptoms and biological changes. It is also complicated by the fact that, if you have PTSD, it increases your chances of developing additional disorders such as problems of memory and cognition, substance abuse, depression, and other physical and mental problems. The disorder can also impair your ability to function in family or social life, and can lead to such problems as marital problems and divorces, occupational instability, difficulties in parenting and family discord. Fortunately, PTSD is curable through psychotherapy. The problem is that many people are not aware that they are suffering from PTSD, or do not even seek treatment. This book will help you to understand PTSD better and know how you can be treated.

PTSD And Veterans

Service members and veterans returning from conflicts in Afghanistan and Iraq often deal with the side effects of their combat experience way long after leaving the battlefield and coming home to their loved ones. Victims of terror acts, calamities, and other catastrophes also experience lingering mental effects of the trauma after the event.

According to the Veterans Affairs, up to sixteen percent of veterans who served in Afghanistan and Iraq after 9/11 experience PTSD. This is coupled by the fact that many people may experience PTSD symptoms without even knowing it, and may be reluctant to seek for help. Friends and families are usually the first ones to notice changes in a loved one. After coming home, you may often feel on edge, irritable, easily startled, have flashbacks of the trauma, be susceptible to violent and angry outbursts, sleep less and feel fatigued. You can also become numb, indifferent, depressed and lose interest in things you used to enjoy, as well as your family life. It is common for most PTSD sufferers to have trouble getting along with family and friends. The VA has an established system to take care of people exhibiting symptoms of PTSD. Here, you are offered access to low cost mental health therapists, as well as other benefits and then referred to support group. Some of the most important elements of this system are therapy, the use of their facilities, and prescription medication.

However, there is one crucial, but overlooked aspect in dealing with PTSD – home health care and community support. Of course, a competent medical professional or PTSD therapist will have a program designed for you, but if you do not follow through in the community and at home, it will be for nothing. On the other hand, while it is crucial to engage in formal support groups, your friends and family should be your ultimate support group.

The problem is that caregiver stress is frequent among family members who are usually hurt, either mentally or physically, or drained from the experience. In fact, Post Traumatic Stress Disorder has been shown to be distractive enough to cause havoc in families such that they are rendered unable to help each other effectively. If the burden becomes too much, you can consider some home care services. These services provide personal care assistants to give the caregiver a boost as you 'recharge your batteries'. These people are trained, and can be available to provide emotional support and talk to. Having the opportunity to share experiences and vent out feelings is important if you are suffering from depression and PTSD.

On the other hand, if you are not available as a family caregiver, you could miss some warning signs of PTSD that warrant attention such as worsening depression, increasing anxiety, hallucinations, missing medications, or intent harm on others or self, or even overt criminal activity and acts.

Chapter 2: The 7 Reasons You Still Have Ptsd Symptoms

Are you struggling with symptoms like anxiety, hyper-vigilance, painful memories, terrible nightmares, depression, avoidance and disgraceful ideas and feelings? These are a set of symptoms that can make life unhappy and might be brought on by post-traumatic stress disorder (PTSD). Anyone can develop this complication following a traumatic event.

There are many reasons that PTSD symptoms might continue gradually. Here are some possible reasons you or someone you care about may still be suffering.

1. You've tried therapy, and it didn't work.

Many well-meaning therapists have the ability to help somewhat with PTSD signs, but might not be trained in or using the most reliable techniques. Even so, in recent decades, the mental health field has almost refined some types of treatment that are shown to work. While they might not solve all of life's problems, repeated research programs they minimize the absolute worst of PTSD signs for many people, normally within 2 to 4 months. For grownups, these include cognitive processing therapy, extended direct exposure and Eye Movement Desensitization and Reprocessing.

2. You tried several of the treatments from # 1 and it still didn't work.

While these therapies, if properly provided, work for many people, there are always exceptions in any treatment. You may be an outlier (which just means different methods would work better for you). That is where alternative treatments become key, because everybody's brain is a bit different. You may try alternative approaches like expressive therapies, movement, or mindfulness practices, which we'll start checking out in this blog in coming weeks and months.

3. You don't have access to the treatment you really need.

In some cases, it can be hard to find a therapist who is trained in these specialized approaches in your area. If you're having a hard time to find a qualified therapist, look for those positive in providing the therapies listed above.

4. Your trauma is current.

It is pretty common to experience PTSD-like signs during or in the first several weeks following a traumatic memory. The majority of people don't develop complications beyond this point. That's why I don't instantly begin the treatments above with clients if they've just come out of a terrible experience. Rather, we build on natural coping skills and methods to help them make it all the way through this hard time, and stay away from negative coping that's shown to make things worse.

If you have just experienced a traumatic memory, concentrate on resiliency methods like keeping in touch with your normal support system.

5. Avoidance is getting in your way.

Did you know avoidance is one of the main categories of PTSD and typically what fuels it? While staying away from thoughts, memories and feelings associating with bad things that took place seems to make sense and might even be necessary to get through a harmful time, in the long-run it actually makes things even worse. That is because you do not get to process and work through the thoughts and emotions that connect to what happened, and these ideas and emotions, even if they're deep down, develop in a myriad of ways and complicate PTSD.

Sometimes we also stay away from circumstances that remind us of the trauma, or that otherwise feel out of control. Most also avoid treatment or drop out of treatment simply because it ends up being overwhelming. Again all of this makes sense in context, yet can also be reinforcing symptoms. We'll also discuss more about avoiding in future post.

PE specifically targets avoidance, but other treatments also help you gain the self-confidence to deal with challenging (but physically safe) circumstances, ideas and feelings.

6. The PTSD is making you be very hard on yourself.

At times, people with PTSD blame themselves incorrectly for what happened, take on too much blame or embarrassment relating to the situation, or actually believe they're forever and ever harmed by the trauma. This can further be complex in a civilization that tends to blame victims for things like sexual assault (there's a lot more to check out here). While self-blaming thoughts are common and typical, they keep us from moving forward. One of the treatments I pointed out earlier, CPT, particularly targets these ideas that perpetuate PTSD. For many clients, this laser method works quickly, and if they stick with it for several weeks, they find relief.

7. You really need a medical diagnosis upgrade.

If you've been detected with PTSD in the past, you may incorrectly really believe you still have it when there may be something else going on (such as general anxiety or a physical condition). Periodically people might also get an inaccurate diagnosis in the first place. A skilled therapist or psychiatrist can help you sort through what's going on now.

Even if you've struggled with PTSD for many months or years, it does not mean you need to accept these symptoms forever. Like with a physical problem, at times you need to keep searching for a clinician, treatment or alternative approach that is right for you. PTSD is set of signs in reaction to a severe trauma-- it is not something you were born with and you don't have to live with it forever.

Chapter 3: How Ptsd Occurs & Diagnosing It

Not all people who undergo traumatic events develop PTSD and so it cannot be concluded that traumatic experiences in general can cause PTSD. So how does PTSD occur?

Traumatic events are only factors that trigger PTSD. The experience of traumatic events causes an adrenaline response that creates neurological patterns inside one's brain. These patterns last for a long time after a traumatic experience and makes the person hyper-reactive to the presence of fearful stimuli. With the experience of traumatic events and reliving these, stress hormones are being secreted that depress the activities of the hypothalamus and thus contribute to the development of PTSD. Hormonal imbalances have been found in people with PTSD and are said to contribute to its development. These hormonal imbalances may create a pattern that will make a person develop a maladaptive response to stressful and traumatic experiences.

People suffering from PTSD were also observed to have low levels of serotonin. This now explains why people with PTSD may experience anxiety, aggression, impulsivity, and thoughts of suicide.

People with PTSD and low dopamine levels in the body may show motor deficits, apathy and impaired attention while if people with PTSD have increased levels of dopamine, this may result in restlessness, agitation, and even psychosis.

This is essentially how PTSD occurs. However, the question arises why some people get PTSD while others do not, even if they experience the same event. Not all people get PTSD even if they undergo the same experience because of different factors. These factors are divided into two which are: the risk factors and the resilience factors. The risk factors are those factors that predispose the person to develop PTSD while the resilience factors are the factors that help reduce the risk of PTSD. Here are the factors as being classified:

Risk Factors

History of mental illness

Experiences of dangerous events and traumas

Experiencing or witnessing getting hurt or killed

Having intense fear, a feeling of horror or hopelessness

Less support after the traumatic event

Additional stressful events after the traumatic event

Resilience Factors

Having a support system after the traumatic event

Developing a coping strategy after the traumatic event

Acting and responding effectively even if there is fear and pressure

These are the factors that will help in determining who is predisposed to develop PTSD and giving him or her the necessary assistance to prevent its occurrence.

How is PTSD diagnosed?

Diagnosis of PTSD involves checking for the presence of the signs and symptoms of PTSD, coupled with a thorough psychological evaluation done by a professional. The patient will be asked about the different signs and symptoms that he is experiencing and what led to the occurrence of those symptoms. A medical exam may also be necessary to see if the person has any other medical conditions that may contribute to the signs and symptoms that he has been experiencing.

The Diagnostic and Statistical Manual of Mental Disorders has a set of criteria that serve as a guide in the diagnosis of PTSD. For one to be considered having PTSD, he or she must have the following:

The person experienced or witnessed an event that resulted in death or serious injury or merely being threatened with such.

The person's response to the traumatic event is helplessness, intense fear and horror.

The person is reliving the said event through nightmares, flashbacks or seeing distressing images.

He avoids situations that may pose the same threat or that remind him of the traumatic events.

He is unable to concentrate or he has sleep pattern disturbance due to hyper-alertness.

The symptoms lasted for a month and disturb one's daily living.

If the person has these symptoms, then he may have PTSD. The diagnosis can only be given by a doctor, and thus consultation should be done to properly address the problem that the person is experiencing.

Chapter 4:Preventing Ptsd After Trauma

Of course, knowing the symptoms is only the first step. The word trauma actually comes from a Greek word which means "wound". Inasmuch as physical wounds and injuries can be treated with first aid to prevent things from getting worse, there are things you can do to mitigate PTSD.

In this instance, the person you're treating has just experienced something traumatic and is yet to be diagnosed to have PTSD. Your goal here is to make sure it never gets to that point. You do this by not only helping the person cope with the stress that he or she would otherwise not be able to take on alone, but also by providing means to prepare for stress in the near future.

The first thing that needs to be done is to meet all of the person's immediate needs, which will vary on a case to case basis. For example, those who have had their homes wrecked by calamities will need food, shelter, and clothing. People who just lost their jobs will need some way of supporting themselves while they find another one. Because you are likely to be a close friend or family member, you may be able to provide some of these personally. If not, you can offer moral support and connect the person to those who can.

Not many people know it, but support groups for people who are undergoing troubles are within arm's reach. You can go online, to your local hospital or a special government agency, your community, and even your local church. The bigger challenge is getting the one that best suits the person who needs it. Try to work out what is best for the person by choosing an option that helps but doesn't put too much pressure on him or her.

The next thing you will want to do is to help the person relax. Even the most comfortable bed won't protect a traumatized individual from losing sleep. When left alone, people who have had negative experiences won't stop thinking about what just happened, and this will cause both physical and mental strains on them. The best way to deal with this is to distract them and help them keep more pleasant thoughts in their heads. Certain forms of physical therapy can also help, but sometimes even the mere presence of friends and loved ones alone does wonders.

In line with the steps above, you also need to make sure that the person stays healthy. Stress can significantly damage one's appetite, which is never good. Make sure the person maintains a proper diet and gets adequate exercise or physical activity.

The next thing to do is to teach the person self-help. You won't always be there to help deal with the recurring trauma and stress, so the long-term method of preventing PTSD is to teach him or her how to cope with the effects of trauma on their own. This includes teaching relaxation techniques and finding reliable support group sessions that the person can attend on his or her own.

Studies have shown that maintaining a journal can help a person sort out fears and emotions. This is great advice for people who are experiencing nightmares or don't have others to share their fears with all the time. Sometimes people need to see their own experiences detached from themselves (in the form of a journal) to have a bird's eye view of what they are going through.

In line with the above, educating the person about PTSD is also very important. The person you're treating needs to know the nature of trauma and what he or she could possibly experience because awareness allows them to detach themselves from what they are going through so that they are able to get on with their lives as usual.

Remember that trauma also affects a person emotionally. Therefore, doing anything that can help a person feel better after a terrible experience can definitely help them out. For example, taking time to talk to the person in order to reassure him or her can make a lot of difference. The idea is to make the person feel less helpless and vulnerable, and to aid in the realization that life still goes on.

One thing that you should do is to avoid triggering flashbacks although there are times when this might be useful. As such, they should only be done in a controlled environment (i.e. in the hands of a doctor). Generally, however, if you know what causes a person anxiety, find ways to make his/her exposure to it minimal, if it cannot be totally avoided.

Finally, remember that preventing the effects of trauma takes time. This means that you need to keep in touch with the person because they need someone supportive and trusted, and it's likely that you have to play that part for him or her. You don't always have to be physically there all the time, but you need to be available in case of emergencies. Letting the person know you are always available and giving him/her contact details will do. In fact, the act of giving that person a means of contacting you when needed is a form of security in itself.

If done properly, the steps above would significantly reduce the chances of any stress induced by trauma turning into PTSD. Even if it does go to that extent, it won't be as severe, making it easier to handle in the long run.

Chapter 5: Move Mountains: Healing Powers Of Movement To Cope With Ptsd

"She took a step and didn't want to take any more, but she did."
— Markus Zusak, The Book Thief

Based on Chapter 3's insights and options about holistic PTSD treatments available for you, Chapter 4 will now briefly validate why movement and exercise can move mountains as far as restoring your holistic health, happiness, confidence, sleep, sanity, peace, and healing from PTSD.Since so many books, gyms, and local recreation centers presently focus on diverse forms of movement and accommodating, fun exercises to address all ages, body types, interests, needs, and lifestyles, this chapter will merely overview a few additional ideas. Stop sitting on the sofa and lounging in your hammock. Curb your couch potato habits for more holistic health with me today in a mindful way.

As the Zuzak quote above infers, I admit how it is surely arduous to take those initial steps. Whether you want to dance, skate, stroll, scoot, golf, kick, spin, or jog, movement is something so natural and free that can expedite your ability to regain control, confidence, health, and serenity from complex PTSD.

Why and how does movement buffer against PTSD? Findings by Dick, Niles, Street, DiMartino, & Mitchell (2014) further insist how low- to moderate-intensity body-awareness movement activities (such as Pilâtes, yoga, therapeutic dance, tai chi or qi gong), can greatly reduce symptoms of anxiety and depression and have produced positive results in PTSD sufferers (p. 1170). To illustrate, I recently took a form of Indonesian marital arts class called Silat, which not only taught various self-protection mechanisms but was also rooted deeply in mindfulness techniques. What are some physical ways to move and groove more mindfully today? Simply opting for stairs over elevators can be a great start for those initial baby steps!

Why is movement so essential to regaining control of your life from complex PTSD in the technical and therapeutic sense? Without getting too medical mumbo jumbo on you, physical activity can counter the toxic build-up from excessive cortisol and other stress accumulation that you have been pummeled with from trauma over time. Girdwain & Mcgee (2013) specifically acknowledge in Health how the therapeutic role of fitness for mental health is integral: "A proven way to ease anxiety naturally is with a bout of cardio, says Michael Otto, PhD, co-author of Exercise for Mood and Anxiety. Getting your heart pumping increases the release of mood-stabilizing neurotransmitters, like serotonin, norepinephrine and GABA, which is why you can feel like you're sweating off stress during Spinning class" (p. 47). Step class or trampoline time, anyone? Roller-skating or rollerblading party?

"The past can teach us, nurture us, but it cannot sustain us. The essence of life is change, and we must move ever forward or the soul will wither and die."
— Susanna Kearsley, <u>Mariana</u>

Another reason to break a sweat against PTSD is because exercise also serves as a PTSD stress-buffer and way to move forward from the past. Kearsley's quote is a great affirmation for these skills to "move" ahead and recover mindfully. In fact, movement is further linked to positive impacts on the decrease of symptoms associated with depression, PTSD, and a host of others, according to various studies (Dick, Niles, Street, DiMartino, & Mitchell, 2014, p. 1170). Find that water bottle and bust a mindful move today!

Lastly, are you wondering how much is enough as far as movement? Girdwain &

Mcgee (2013) encourage us to aim for 150 minutes per week of moderate activity (p. 47).Salsa or Zumba this weekend? Hip hop class or Bhangra Masala at the YMCA?

ABCS of Movement Activity

Consider adding some of these ABCs of movement ideas to your life to battle complex PTSD more mindfully. This activity also exercises your brain and creativity. It jogs and boots your memory to add more variety. Are you ready to **move mountains** holistically?

Aerobics

Badminton, biking, boxing, and bowling

Cricket and cycling

Dancing and diving

E_____

Football

Golfing and gardening

Hula hooping and hiking

I_____

J_____

Karate, Kung fu

L_____

M_____

N_____

O_____

Pilates

Q_____

R_____

Self-defense classes, skating, and swimming

T_____

U_____

Volleyball

Walking

X_____

Yoga

Zumba, ziplining

Now it is your turn to fill in the blanks. Add to the list to make your own ABCs of Movement work for you! Keep this list and celebrate the risks and efforts that you take as you find new ways to move and groove against complex PTSD with play and movement.

Child's Play: Although yoga will be featured in the mindfulness section in Chapter 8, I wanted to highlight yoga's restorative child pose, one of my personal favorites to fight PTSD. Its name is quite fitting in my case since my PTSD emerged during exposure to childhood trauma in my household.

Child's pose is quite easy for all levels: "Sit on shins with hips resting on heels. Lay chest on thighs and relax with forehead to floor. Hold for 8 to 10 breaths" (Girdwain & Mcgee, 2013, p. 47). It is so great for your body, mind, and spirit! It makes me feel super safe, too, something that is often a major issue with complex PTSD. Try it today without diaper changes or bottle feeding-yay! If you need visuals or videos, search online today and find that Zen!

Twist and Shout: Of course the famous song can automatically release stress, but this tip is related to supine twists in yoga. This one is adaptable for all levels and body types as you draw in your knees close toward your chest. Then place your right hand on your left knee, and extend your left arm straight out to the left. Inhale, and as you exhale, roll your knees to the right. Take a few deliberate breaths here. Next, inhale and draw your knees back to center, and exhale as you squeeze them back in toward your chest.

Studies claim how "This pose is also effective at relieving tension in the lower back, where many of us carry stress" (Eichenseher, 2016, p. 69). Learn to let go, twist, and shout for resilience against complex PTSD!

Again, feel free to search online for a ton of free videos and visuals to guide your twister action!

Warrior Way: Warrior pose, as its name implies, is also fabulous a stress reliever and major empowering movement in yoga. Simply step out sideways on your mat so your feet are about 3 to 4 feet apart as you press your feet into the ground and maintain navel support. Then turn out your right leg and foot out to the right. Turn your back leg and foot slightly and then align your right heel with the arch of your left foot.

Experts praise it for grounding work as you can "Really plant onto the earth through your feet and legs. Inhale and reach your arms out to the sides; exhale and bend your right knee, and slide your right sitting bone toward your right foot. Be careful not to let your knee go past your ankle.

Stay stable through your back leg—this is a strong and focused posture that requires you to remain in the present moment. Take 5 breaths here. Maintain the supports that keep you grounded. Inhale and push into the earth to straighten your right leg and come out of the posture. Exhale your way back to center. Repeat on your left side" (Eichenseher 2016,p. 70). Get that inner Moana groove on with warrior pose for more mindfulness and healing.

Reflection: Break for a moment and reflect on some insights and "aha" moments from this chapter. Journal about your thoughts, questions, feelings, etc.

Chapter 6: Diagnosing Ptsd

The DSM-IV's narrow definition of PTSD requires that the patient "experience, witness or be confronted with an event that involves actual or threatened death, serious injury or a threat to their physical integrity (such as rape). This trauma must be severe enough to cause intense fear, helplessness or horror." The definition is necessarily narrow and specific so as to differentiate sufferers of PTSD from those who are experiencing emotional upset due to "common everyday experiences that may overwhelm an individual such as feeling "traumatized" by a presentation at work or having to dance in public.The DSM-IV also differentiates PTSD from other conditions involving severe distress." xv

Diagnosing the disorder is difficult because one of the symptoms is avoidance, meaning that the patient is often unwilling to talk about the incident or how it is affecting them. Due to societal pressure that people "deal with" their emotional issues, some doctors or other health professionals might even ignore the signs of PTSD.xvi A patient's symptoms may also be obscured "by depression, substance abuse, or other comorbidities."xvii

To be diagnosed, the patient must present to a doctor or mental health professional, and must "meet criteria spelled out in the Diagnostic and Statistical Manual of Mental Disorders (DSM), published by the American Psychiatric Association. This manual is used by mental health professionals to diagnose mental conditions and by insurance companies to determine reimbursement for treatment."xviiiThe criteria are the symptoms fromChapter 2.

The diagnosing doctor or mental health professional will need to ask non-judgmental questions that are direct and empathetic in order to get an avoidance-sufferer to open up and be willing to discuss the event. Patients who are suffering from PTSD due to some childhood trauma may be especially difficult to draw out for diagnosis.

There is a screening questionnaire for health care professionals to use to help diagnose the disorder.It reportedly has "a sensitivity of 80 percent and a specificity of 97 percent for the diagnosis of PTSD. Examples of the questions include: "Do you have diminished interest in activities"; "Do you have problems sleeping?"; and "Do you find it hard to feel or show affection for others?"" xix

Other questions a doctor will probably ask a patient with possible PTSD include:

"What are your symptoms?

When did you or your loved ones first notice your symptoms?

Have you ever experienced or witnessed an event that was life- threatening to you or someone else?

Have you ever been physically, sexually or emotionally harmed?

Do you have disturbing thoughts, memories or nightmares of the traumayouexperienced?

Do you ever feel as if you are reliving the traumatic event, through flashbacks or hallucinations?

Do you avoid certain people, places or situations that remind you of the traumatic experience?

Have you lost interest in things or felt numb?

Do you feel jumpy, on guard, or easily startled?

Do you frequently feel irritable or angry?

Are you having trouble sleeping?

Is anything happening in your life right now that is making you feel unsafe?

Have you been having any problems at school or work?

Have you been having problems in your personal relationships?

Have you ever thought about harming yourself or others?

Do you drink alcohol or use illegal drugs? How often?

Have you been treated for other psychiatric symptoms or mental illness in the past? If yes, what type of therapy was most beneficial?" xx

If you encounter a massage client who is experiencing symptoms after a trauma, direct him or her to their doctor. Advise the client to write down their symptoms, and how long they've been experiencing them, as well as their medical history, to take with them to the appointment. That way, if the doctor begins asking questions that the client does not want to answer because of trauma, there will be a written record. xxi

Chapter 7: True Stories Of Spiritual Encounters

Now, the reason why I'm about to share these very real stories is to introduce you to the real possibility that PMDS and PTSD is an entity. Due to your religious background you may not believe such things are possible, but I'm here to tell you firsthand that they are. In order for these things that I am about to show you to work, you must at lease have an open mind to the possibility. Another revelation of this possibility is that PMDS and PTSD is nothing but an invisible terrorist. I was told that these entities were called upon by the Arabic military leaders to help fight against Americans. Further proof of this statement appeared on **television on 11-11-15, episode 51 of a program called**

"Paranormal Witness". Beneath the rock series special: no military training prepare eight US Marines for the ghostly enemy they encounter at the outpost in Afghanistan. I recommend you go and watch this. If you are still having doubts about what I'm saying, after watching this episode, I'm sure you won't.

My next-door neighbor is of the Muslim faith and he and his family are from an Arabic country, and are now US citizens. He told me that in his country they believe in praying to jinns for protection and favors. He said as a little boy he was introduced to the idea of praying to the jinns through his grandfather. He said that his grandfather used to sit, pray, and talk to these invisible beings as if they were actually there. My neighbor said that he has witnessed his grandfather several times asking them for their protection for his family as they traveled about the country.

He also said that his grandfather told him that you can also ask the jinns to seek justice for you in the form of vengeance. He said that you could summon them if anyone ever stole something of yours, or tried to harm you or your family, but that you would have to give them some type of offering. I asked my neighbor where these entities live. He said that most of them live in caves, in the desert, vacant houses, abandoned buildings, and some lakes.

He also told me that these entities must be treated with the utmost respect, and that some of them are very dangerous, tricky, powerful, and evil. But there are those that can be very nice and helpful, and those are the only ones that you must contact. But the majority of them don't like humans so he does not recommend people to work with them without the proper knowledge and training.

He went on to say that the evil jinns can appear to you in a very deceptive form, such as a passed loved one, or even an ascended master. He then said that jinns are very territorial and that they will defend their land with a vengeance of force for a lifetime in the form of a generational curse.

One day at work I became friends with a guy that was just hired, he had recently moved here from the middle east, Afghanistan to be exact. He was in his early 40s, a father of four, and was a very hard worker. One day out of the blue we started talking about war and the long term effects it has on the person and their families. He told me that most Arabic countries had a secret weapon they use on their enemies, especially the USA. I said really, can you tell me or is it forbidden? He said it is forbidden but he would tell me because he was against any kind of war or destruction. I said OK what is it, he said it was jinns, you call them demons or the fallen angels.

Then he went on to tell me in great detail how his culture respected them, asked them for favors, protection and even worshiped them. He also said that if you come on to their land without their consent, you and your family would be cursed forever until you appease them. Then he asked me if I had ever been in the military and been involved in any wars overseas.

I said yes and no. I went on to tell him my story of how I was in the army at the time of the gulf war. I was not deployed there but my ex-wife was. He said I'll bet she had problems physically and mentally when she returned right? I said yes, she was diagnosed with PTSD. He then said yes that's what your people call it but it's not, it's the curse of the jinn, and that I was cursed also.

I said well if you are referring to PTSD, yes I was diagnosed with it also upon my exit of the military. I said OK let's say I do have the curse, how do I break it and get rid of the jinn. He said that the only way to break the curse and get rid of it forever, would be to go back to that country into the exact desert which my feet or my wife's feet first touch the sand, apologize and ask for forgiveness and give a peace offering of a particular kind.

Then wait till they appear in the sand as a twirling wind (a dust devil or tornado as we call them). I then asked him what to do if that's not possible for me or anyone else that is suffering from PTSD to go back there, what else can I do? He said you can have someone else go there on your wife's behalf to present the offering. Do you happen to know a person from that country that will be returning in the near future and that you trust? I said no sir I don't, is there another option? He said yes you can control the jinn keep them at bay and protect you and your family.

He told me I could use certain powerful crystals, certain scents, herbs, sounds, music, and a particular incense and medallion, in a particular order that would ward off the entity that was associated with the curse. Now with all of this being told to me I still didn't believe it 100% yet. I'm the type of person that will listen to what you have to say with an open mind and no judgment, because everyone has the right to say and believe in what they choose.

But before I'm on board with you 100% I have to do my own research into the subject at hand and let my gut feeling guide me to the truth, and that I did. Over the next several years I was dedicated in finding out more about the jinns and the PTSD curse, and a cure. Through my own research I have found out that what was told to me was accurate. I found stories in the bible, the koran, the torah, and in the Hebrew and Judaism culture about the jinns and their effects on people. I've also discovered that the eastern world and the Christians in particular, do not believe in the jinns. They believe that it is just a fairytale or folklore that does not exist.

I believe that not only do jinns exist, but they are here and are the ones that are making the rules and running the country. I also found out that they go by other names such as the demiurge, illuminati, reptilians or their most common name, demons. These entities are everywhere, they also walk among us, and most people don't even recognize them, because, they are also shape shifters and can look like humans, or animals especially dogs and cat.

You can easily identify them if you know their characteristics and behavior. You can also destroy them, control them or keep them away from you, your family and pets, which I will discuss in a later addition.

Now I am the type of person that knows how to listen to my gut feeling, and it was telling me this could be real and that there is a connection here to our soldiers having PTSD. I love researching something, especially if it stirs my gut feeling, then it's worth researching. I researched jinns, their origins, their characteristics etc., and found out they are real.

The old testament the Koran and the torah speak of them often. The torah states that these beings were created from smokeless fire by God, before he created man, and that they have been here living on earth in an invisible parallel realm, way before mankind was created.

The 22 chapters of the bible that were taken out of today's bible version, (the King James version) spoke very commonly of the jinns. It said that the jinns were the fallen angels, and that God banished them here to earth to live in an alternate reality, separate from mankind (in other words an invisible plane).

They have been called by many different names such as spirits, ghosts, shadow people, and ghouls. In the western society they're mostly called demons.

Over the next several months of my research on these entities, I came to find out that ancient Egyptians called them gods, and they were called upon frequently, for favors and protection. The Egyptians also said these entities were dangerous and very tricky, just like my neighbor had previously said.

They also said that the priests which were the chosen ones, were only allowed to summon and work with them. I also discovered that it is believed by many cultures that God made them first before he made man. It was also believed that jinns were very greedy, selfish, and hard for God to control. It was also said that when God made man and said that we were his greatest creation the jinns became very jealous.

And when God told them to serve us they became very angry, and told God that they will not bow down and serve man because they were created first and they were better. So with that final defiance to

God he threw them out of heaven and banned them forever. The leader of the jinns declared war against man and God and this is where we get the term evil, dark energy, etc.

It is believed that they have families and live lives similar to ours. It is also said that they have a government, officials, community leaders and technology that is light-years above our own, and even an army with a chain of command such as ours.

Whether this is all true or not I'm not sure, but I do believe it holds some validity. It is also said that they tend to live in the desert, in caves, old abandoned buildings, lakes, oceans and houses that have been vacant for a long period of time.

Chapter 8: Conditioning Of Yourself

It is widely evident that recovery from PTSD is a gradual process. Healing does not happen overnight and the memories of the trauma will never disappear. But here are some more tips on preparing yourself to recover from the disorder.

First: Do not be ashamed to seek support

PTSD will make you feel disconnected from your friends and family. It will tempt you to withdraw from social life altogether. This should never be allowed under any circumstances. One of the vital aspects of your recovery is the support of others. Therefore, you need to reach out to friends and family and ask for it.

If this support is not enough, contact support groups and join people like you, who are suffering from the same sort of disorder. They will help you release any feelings of isolation and loneliness. They will also give you critical information on how to deal with your situation.

Second: Challenge what you perceive as helplessness

PTSD is a synonym of helplessness. The trauma you experienced left you with feelings of powerlessness and vulnerability. You need to remind yourself that once you were a strong person with the ability to cope through rough times. You need to persuade yourself to become that person again.

The best way to do this is to volunteer to help others. Give blood, make a donation, or help a friend. Do everything it takes to challenge the feeling that you are helpless. You are not. But you need to convince yourself of that.

Third: Get out to nature

Hiking, camping, biking, climbing, rafting, skiing and all other outdoor activities will gorge your body full of natural endorphins.

Add this to the relaxation, seclusion and peace of the natural environment and you will be relaxed enough to persuade your nervous system to get unstuck and move on.

Fourth: Train your loved ones to help you

The support of your family is crucial. In number one, you needed to ask for their support. Now you need to show them how they can support you. You should explain to them that:

☐ They should be patient.

Recovery will take time. The pace may be slow but they need to offer a sympathetic ear which will speed things up. They also need to gently tell you to stop living in the past and move on.

☐ They should try to prepare and anticipate possible triggers.

Anniversary dates, people and places associated with the event, sights, sounds, or smells can bring back the ugly memories. They should know and knowledge always provides better support.

☐ The symptoms of PTSD are not to be taken personally.

At first your symptoms will be indifference, anger and withdrawal. You need to let them know that this has nothing to do with them or their relationship to you.

☐ They should not pressure you into talking

Another of the symptoms is the avoidance of the discussion for the traumatizing event. You may be one of the cases that talking about it could make things even worse if you are not well prepared. You need to let them know that you will do it when the right times comes.

Chapter 9: Symptoms Of Ptsd In Children

Just like in a lot of other things, children and teens may react and handle the aftermath of trauma in entirely different ways. Symptoms of Post-Traumatic Stress Disorder (PTSD) in children include the following:

Fear of being separated from and being unusually clingy to parents or guardians

Acting out the traumatic event through play or demonstrating it through drawings and stories

Losing the ability to talk and other previously-acquired skills, such as using the toilet

Experiencing body aches and pains even with no evident cause

Nightmares and other sleeping problems

Bad temper and aggression

Emergence of new phobias, such as fear of monsters

It is entirely understandable to experience upsetting and distressing feelings after being involved with or after witnessing a traumatic event. However, if these problems last longer than a month, and are very severe, Post-Traumatic Stress Disorder (PTSD) may already be diagnosed and it is then very imperative that the individual seek professional medical help.

Causes and Risk Factors of PTSD

We all have a unique capacity to handle and cope with whatever life throws in our way and along with this uniqueness is our very own way on how to manage fear, stress, and trauma. Each individual is known to react to certain traumatic events differently and while most people will probably experience a certain kind of trauma at some point in life, it is important to know that not all traumatic experiences necessarily result to Post-Traumatic Stress Disorder (PTSD).

Unfortunately, up to these days, doctors cannot pinpoint the very reason as to why some people who go through traumatic events develop PTSD while some others do not. However, while it is considered unattainable to precisely know who will develop Post-Traumatic Stress Disorder (PTSD) in response to experiencing a certain traumatic event, there are certain factors which could increase a person's risk of developing the disorder.

Just like most mental health problems, researchers believe that the development of PTSD is linked to the interplay of certain factors and components. The following factors are considered to play a major role in significantly increasing a person's risk of developing PTSD or in making symptoms much more severe:

Repeated, prolonged, or intense trauma

Other previous traumatic events experienced earlier in life

Having a family history of PTSD, depression, anxiety and other mental health problems

The kind of temperament the individual has

History of experiencing other mental health problems, such as depression or anxiety

Lacking a good support system from family, friends and other loved ones

Experiencing high levels of stress daily

Dealing with extra stress after the trauma, such as loss of a loved one or experiencing injury

Once again, not everyone who goes through a traumatic and distressing experience automatically develops PTSD. It is very important to hold on to the point that in order to be able to decrease your chances of developing this disorder, it is very vital to develop good and strong coping strategies for all the stressors of your daily life and to be able to build a strong support system from your family and loved ones.

Available Treatment Options for PTSD

If you believe that you or someone you deeply care about is suffering from Post-Traumatic Stress Disorder (PTSD), it is highly recommended to seek professional medical help immediately.

The various distressing symptoms that accompany PTSD could greatly affect different important aspects of your life. It could considerably interfere with your family life and your relationships and could even lead to more serious health problems which in turn, could further cause deterioration in the overall quality of your life.

Thus, as much as possible, see to it that you are able to deal with the problem while it is still early. Making an effort to face the issue now could make a great deal of difference towards preventing the problem from getting worse and from further inflicting even more damage to your life in general.

The primary goals of the available treatment options for Post-Traumatic Stress Disorder (PTSD) include trying to reduce the physical and emotional symptoms accompanying the disorder, improve the ability to function daily, heal broken relationships and repair other damaged life aspects, and hopefully to help the person not just cope with the disorder but to completely overcome it eventually as well.

The different available treatment types for PTSD include the following:

PSYCHOTHERAPY

Psychotherapy is a kind of talk therapy which particularly aims to help the individual not just in managing the accompanying symptoms of the disorder but most importantly, in helping to discover the underlying causes of the persistent fear and in developing strategies on how to best deal with these fears and consequently overcome them.

Some of the leading psychotherapy approaches include the following:

Trauma-Focused Cognitive-Behavioral Therapy (CBT)

Cognitive-behavioral therapy is a therapy which aims to examine and correct negative thought patterns and behaviors which could lead to intense feelings of anxiety. It is primarily based on the concept that instead of being controlled by external situations, it is your very own thoughts that considerably influence the way you feel and consequently behave.

Once you are able to recognize and correct existing negative thoughts and perceptions, you could then try to find more productive ways on how to react, feel, and consequently, behave.

Exposure Therapy

Exposure therapy is a certain kind of therapy which helps allow individuals who suffer from PTSD to face their fears and eventually gain more control of it. Performed in a safe and well-controlled environment with a therapist, the person is exposed to certain objects or situations which could trigger fear and anxiety in order for the individual to confront the fear, gradually get used to it, and eventually overcome it fully.

Instead of continuously avoiding and suppressing your fears and emotions, exposure therapy allows you to develop skills on how to confront and better deal with your fears and anxiety in a safe and gradual manner. It will teach you how to build more confidence in the face of your fear which in turn, will allow you to gain back control over your entire life.

Exposure therapy is typically used along with cognitive-behavioral therapy in order to be able to attain more productive results.

Eye Movement Desensitization and Reprocessing (EMDR)

Eye Movement Desensitization and Reprocessing is a complex type of psychotherapy which is primarily intended to stimulate the information processing system of the brain. In this therapy, the individual will make rhythmic and guided eye movements while recollecting certain aspects of the traumatic event.

The therapy incorporates certain aspects of cognitive-behavioral therapy with eye movements or other types of rhythmic stimulation which help awaken the information processing system of the brain, a certain area of the brain which is disrupted when under severe stress. This in turn, could help you process the trauma that happened in a more efficient manner and promote the speeding up of the recovery process.

FAMILY THERAPY

Post-Traumatic Stress Disorder (PTSD) could both affect you and people who are close to you, most especially your family. And since it is never easy to carry the burdens of PTSD all alone, it is very important to acknowledge the fact that you will need all the support you can get.

Family therapy is considered to be a very productive approach towards helping an individual overcome PTSD and many other disorders and health conditions for that matter. Being your major support system, your family needs to understand what precisely you are going through and this type of therapy could do exactly that.

It is considered very helpful in allowing every family member to adjust to the changes going on inside the person suffering from the disorder, maintain good communication, and most importantly, to address and solve relationship problems which have been inflicted by the various distressing symptoms of PTSD.

All these are known to be very vital not just for the recovery of the family member who suffers from the disorder itself, but also for the emotional healing of loved ones who have also suffered the aftermath of PTSD.

MEDICATIONS

Medications are not typically considered as a first-line treatment for Post-Traumatic Stress Disorder (PTSD). However, they may be prescribed as a part of your treatment in order to control certain symptoms of PTSD and to make it easier to go through and get the most out of psychotherapy.

Two medications which have been approved to alleviate symptoms of PSTD among adults are sertraline (Zoloft) and paroxetine (Paxil), both of which are antidepressants. They are known to help stabilize mood, lessen sleeping problems, and help control other symptoms such as extreme anxiety and worry.

However, in spite of their valuable properties, it is very important to be fully aware of the fact that taking these medicines and other similar drugs could carry unpleasant side effects. Thus, it is very important to take these medications only under the supervision of a healthcare professional.

Do not hesitate to discuss important matters with your doctor or therapist first before pursuing any treatment option. People may respond to varying forms of treatment differently and what works best for a certain person may not have the same effect to another. As such, it is very important that you are able to find the kind of treatment which will match your specific needs, generate the most productive results, and help take you towards the road to healing and towards gaining back control over your life in the best way.

Self-help Tips on How to Successfully Overcome Post-Traumatic Stress Disorder (PTSD)

The effects of traumatic events do not just stop at the physical damages that they typically cause. Apart from the physical harm, the most difficult impact of a terrifying and traumatic event lies in the deep emotional and psychological wounds that they inflict on the individual. The aftermath of trauma usually leaves a person with intense and extremely distressing thoughts and emotions which in turn, could further result to more damage to other important life aspects.

Recovering from all the injuries brought by the trauma will certainly take time and it will be difficult to repair your shattered sense of security, make your emotions stable, and be able to build your life once again. While seeking professional medical help is highly advised for your guided recovery, know that you yourself also have the power to make a great deal of difference towards helping yourself feel better and making the healing process possible and successful.

On Making Positive Changes within Yourself

It all starts within. As such, if you want to make some positive changes in the different aspects of your life after the trauma has caused devastation, you must first start to make positive changes within yourself.

Here are some valuable self-help tips on how you can successfully make the necessary, helpful changes within yourself in order to gradually heal yourself from the damages inflicted by Post-Traumatic Stress Disorder (PTSD):

Acknowledge and accept your emotions.

It is only natural to feel all kinds of upsetting and distressing emotions after the occurrence of a traumatic event. And at the same, it is completely understandable if you want to suppress these unpleasant feelings instead of facing them head on.

However, no matter how much you want to deny or hold these feelings back and just forget them completely if possible, it is important to know that acknowledging these emotions instead of keeping them locked away is a very necessary part of your healing process.

Acknowledge your emotions. Allow yourself to feel what you feel deep inside. And consequently, make an effort to gradually accept these feelings. Only then will you be able to start moving forward towards the road to healing.

Take responsibility.

While the traumatic event that has occurred to you is something that is beyond your control and something that you certainly cannot be liable about, you must recognize the fact that how you handle your emotions and your behavior after the trauma is now your full responsibility.

Yes, it would be easier to blame someone, anyone. But that would not take you anywhere. Sure, you can give yourself time to feel all the negative emotions that are swirling inside you but not to the point that they start taking over your life. Remember, it is justifiable to feel down and shattered after the trauma. But getting out of being stuck is a decision that you have to make.

Gain back control by taking full responsibility of your thoughts and your actions. Start being in charge once again with every aspect of your life, little by little. This sense of control will do a great deal of difference in making your confidence whole and strong once more.

Open yourself up and reach out to others for support.

Suffering from PTSD is a difficult and an extremely heavy burden to carry on your own. While the effects of this disorder could make you feel emotionally cut off from your loved ones, know that you are not in this battle alone and that being reconnected to your loved ones and to life in general is a very essential aspect towards your recovery.

The numbness that you feel, all the negative emotions, and the shattered sense of safety, may make it easy for you to withdraw from your relationships and from participating in social activities. Instead of giving in to this temptation, make an effort to reach out to others instead, for support and just for the mere joy and comfort of being with others you care about and care for you in return, both of which are vital for your emotional healing.

Here are some things which you can do in order to reconnect with others and establish healthy relationships once again:

Spend quality time with loved ones and do common and ordinary things with other people, activities which have nothing to do with the tragedy or trauma. Aside from rebuilding relationships broken by the trauma, spending time with others will also help rekindle old interests which will be greatly beneficial for reawakening your sense of self.

Talk to someone close to you about your feelings. Open yourself up and have the courage to share what you have been through. Doing so will help release pent up emotions and may help you come to terms with the unpleasant experience.

Talk to other individuals who share similar experiences. This will significantly help in making you feel less isolated. Also, hearing success stories on how others are able to cope with and even overcome PTSD can help give inspiration for you to win this difficult battle.

Be patient with yourself.

Everyone has their own pace of healing. As such, you must keep yourself reminded that recovery is something you just could not attain overnight. Be patient with yourself and give yourself time to do what you have to do. Take it one step at a time. Remember, every small step and every little progress will make you closer to your goal.

Live in the present moment.

Instead of dwelling on what you have lost because of the incident, focus instead on what you do have now. As you keep mourning over what has happened in the past or as you keep worrying about what the future might hold, you unconsciously let life slip away.

Instead of letting your thoughts be overwhelmed by the regrets of the past or worries about the future, learn to experience life right here and right now.

If you are taking a shower, for instance, instead of constantly thinking about what happened or what might happen, focus instead on what is happening now. Feel the coolness of the water on your skin, take pleasure in how the soap softly lathers, and enjoy the scent of your favorite shampoo.

Be aware of every present moment. Be mindful of every single feeling or experience it holds for it is with each of these little moments that life is lived and life will be made of. Not only will living in the present give you more sense of peace, it will allow you to recognize and appreciate all the little things that you do have as well.

Overcome feelings of helplessness by extending help to others.

Trauma has its very own way of leaving you feeling extremely weak and helpless. Overcome these feelings of helplessness by helping others in a lot of different ways - reach out to a friend in need, comfort a loved one, make some donations to a certain charity, donate blood, and awaken your sense of volunteerism.

By helping others, you will significantly realize that not all is lost considering that you still have got something to give. Lending a hand and making contributions even in small ways will allow you to reclaim your sense of power and control, a very huge step towards overcoming PTSD.

If you are suffering from Post-Traumatic Stress Disorder (PTSD), making these positive changes within yourself may be extremely hard and may even feel unattainable at times. However, know that despite the difficulty is the full possibility that you can make these changes happen. Hold on to this little hope. What you need to do now is to make the decision of taking that little, difficult, yet very significant first step that will start your journey towards healing.

Chapter 10: Explosive Anger

Eggshells.If anyone has ever said they "feel like they are walking on eggshells around you," you may have explosive anger.Explosive anger oftentimes comes as a result of a lot of little triggers that accrue anxiety and tension until, POP! All that energy floods out onto one little unsuspecting door, or wall, or ourselves, or another person.The presence of explosive anger means tension and stress has built up to an unmanageable degree, which gives us clues on how to address it.I remind you there is no one size fits all solution to trauma and no miracle or overnight cures.

The trick to explosive anger is to identify and manage the anxiety inducers in little increments.If we have an intense level of fight-energy in us because we work in aggressive environments or we have abusive partners, we may need to review our life circumstances and make a change.If that change is not possible, desired, or viable, than we apply coping skills to manage the fight-energy and anxiety and overtime explosive anger will drift away as our inner security is restored and sense of empowerment is increased.We no longer have to be victimized by our past and turn into victimizers in our present.As the root of explosive anger is anxiety and "fight-energy," my first approach is to practice TREs (explained in detail in its section), which will release that fight energy broiling inside of us. Additional coping skills are listed below and please have patience with yourself in this process.There will come a time to ask for forgiveness from those we have hurt but now is the time to heal ourselves so we can mean it if and when we do.And again, I do not believe in anger work as a solution to explosive anger, de-escalation is the key, but you need to trust what works for you as well and if that currently works, trust your gut.

- ☐ Coping Skills
- ☐ TRE's
- ☐ Magnesium
- ☐ GABA
- ☐ Bellows Breath

Depersonalization/Derealization

Depersonalization and Derealization (DPRD) on its own is a not very well understood aspect of PTSD or in its own form Depersonalization-derealization disorder. While experiencing this condition, the person can feel as if in a dream world or that they are simply an observer of an unreality, detached from their bodies, emotions, and even thoughts. Pharmaceutical and psychotherapeutic treatments have shown inconsistent results when facing DPRD however when improvements are made in underlying conditions such as anxiety and/or depression, improvements are also seen with DPRD.

Research suggests if not a standalone state, DPRD is brought about by a heightened experience of a variety of symptoms including PTS and ranging across the spectrum of mental health conditions.For our purposes in addressing the DPRD of PTS, we again look to bringing awareness back to our bodies and our current conditions through grounding and mindfulness, and seek to address and cope with the underlying conditions that have brought about an episode or state of DPRD.

☐ Coping Skills

☐ Dedicated Space

☐ Grounding

☐ Bellows Breath

☐ Qi Gong

← LEFT

Return to Contents

Coping & Healing

FREE

Dedicated Space

A dedicated space means exactly that, a place, a room, a basement, or even a closet dedicated solely to your healing practices.If your current living arrangement doesn't allow that, we can dedicate any space we choose as long as we have privacy, safety, access, and security to practice, to pray, to meditate, or practice any of the movement therapies when we need to.

As PTS survivors we know and experience firsthand the power our environment can have over us, fortunately we can also <u>use this power to heal</u>.When we dedicate our space for healing, we signify to ourselves our own importance and the importance of healing.As the kitchen serves our eating needs, our dedicated space will serve our healing needs. With a dedicated space, we take responsibility to ensure we always know we have a safe place to go, and ultimately, as time progresses and we continue to practice healing in our dedicated space, simply going into the room or space, heading towards it, or even thinking about it can shift the chemistry in our bodies and our mood towards a sense of safety.

Bellows Breath

The Bellows Breath is a calm and deep breathing technique.Breathing is a major contributor to our bodies processes, it sounds simple and kind of "duh!" but the truth is not a lot of people have a sense of their breathingand how this simple aspect of our lives can spiral symptomatic episodes into a frenzy.For instance, when triggered or experiencing anxiety we begin to breath short shallow breathes, this in turn starves the mind of oxygen and can escalate unhealthy or confused thinking, while our heart rate races and actually requires more oxygen in an escalated state.With Bellows Breathing, we can counteract some of these processes and at least stalemate the cascade of escalating symptoms from a lack of oxygen.

Bellows Breath is also known as diaphragmatic breathing and will stimulate the vagus nerve, the freeway of the parasympathetic nervous system.**Initial studies** have suggested Vagus nerve stimulation, involving a pacemaker like device, can be an effective treatment for depression and anxiety; while we are not promoting, endorsing or denying this level of treatment, it should be noted that the vagus nerve is stimulated by many methods in this book.One easy trick to stimulate the Vagus nerve is to bathe your tongue in Saliva, just imagine you're sucking on a lemon and allow your mouth to fill with saliva then breathe deeply through your nose for 3 minutes.Simple enough, yet effective.

Practice

Standing comfortably, place your feet shoulder width apart

Relax your tailbone towards the floor and press your shoulders back slightly

Begin to breath towards your hips, allow your belly to fill like a balloon pressing outwards and slowly exhale

Congratulations, that is one version of Bellows Breath!

Resources

3 more Breathing Exercises from Dr. Andrew Weil

Video of 3 Breathing Exercises for Anxiety

Free *Kindle* Breathing Apps That Help Pace Breath (also available on Appstore)

Return to Contents

Grounding

Grounding is method to bring your mind back to your body, back to your present, back to your reality.There are many methods, skills, and suggestions for grounding and as you'll eventually find, many of the practices described here are essentially articulate grounding.A simple google search of "Grounding Techniques" will elicit endless suggestions on how to do this, from sucking a lemon or holding an ice cube to counting and naming all the objects around you.When you do this you are tuning in to your reality.When experiencing symptoms of PTS your mind is tuned in to a different reality, something that no longer exists or has yet to exist and grounding is a physical and conscious effort to pull your mind back into alignment with your present.

The main suggestion I add to grounding is that you utilize a grounding method that is connected to the sense that was harmed by the trauma you are experiencing symptoms of.For instance, if you are re-experiencing verbal abuse or traumatic explosions, your auditory sense has been affected.Therefore, utilize an auditory grounding technique such as a listening to a meditative song, singing along to your favorite song, or gentle self-talk spoken aloud.If you are re-experiencing trauma associated with physical abuse or violence, use a physical soothing method such as a self-hug, going for a massage, or holding a stuffed animal.Of course, there is no single effective method for all, so I urge you to explore all possibilities until you find what fits you, what comforts and calms you back to a peaceful present.

Practice

Identify the sense that is stimulated by PTSD

Visual-EMDR

Sensory-massage, self-hug

Auditory-**binaural beats**, meditation music, self-affirmations

Smell-lavender,

Taste-eat ice or lemon

Choose Grounding Technique which suits and soothes the affected sense.

Resources

Resource section of ***www.healingonashoestring.com***

Mindfulness

Mindfulness is actively seeking your current reality or allowing your current reality to be.PTS is hallmarked by trappings of the past; unresolved guilt, fear, terror, helplessness that stains our lives moment to moment.Mindfulness is the effort to tune in to just what is, currently, freshly, and uniquely every moment.Mindfulness allows the mind and body a channel to the peace and healing that is present all around us right now.

Even though the moment of trauma may have lasted only a few seconds or minutes, it can continue to haunt our lives and drag us down, prompt bad decisions which continue, escalate, and compound the injuries.Mindfulness is an intentional method to tune in to the peaceful reality that is right now, to give our nervous systems a break, and allow respite from our habitual and repetitive minds which often automatically returns to our pain.

There are endless methods to mindfulness and none of them require thought, just practice.You can tune in to reality at any time, reality being exactly what is, right now, directly around you.Sitting at a car light in traffic you can allow yourself to appreciate the way the sun sparkles off the streetlight with the expansive blue sky in the beyond.As you read this eBook, you can bring your consciousness to the feel of the tablet in your hands, the way your body is held by gravity wherever you are seated or lying, and the way your body feels, where there is comfort, where there is tension.Below is a list of several resources to begin a practice of mindfulness and a directory of resources if you particularly like this method and would like further information as it applies to healing.

There is a common misconception that mindfulness meditation involves curling ourselves up like acrobats and chanting funny sounds and this is simply not true.You can and already do practice mindfulness anywhere; walking, running, on the subway, with your family.Any moment in your life where you were completely present, there was nothing but you and the moment, you were experiencing mindfulness.

Practice

Motion Mindfulness

Find a safe place indoors or out, or enter your dedicated space, and breathe a sigh of relief, a deep sigh; a sigh that opens the belly down to the hips.

Remove your shoes and socks, if you're comfortable.

Take a few seconds and become aware of your breathing, its pace, its depth.

Take a step forward with your left foot, breathing IN, allowing reality to greet you at your senses, how does the ground feel under your feet? How does the temperature feel against your skin? Are there sounds? Smells? Take note without noting; just experience.

Take a step forward with your right foot, breathing OUT, allowing reality in at this moment, if there are distractions, allow yourself to be free of them for this moment and just experience.

Continue forward or in a circle as you see fit, this practice is not about a destination but breathing in, and out, each moment with presence.

Congratulations! You have just practiced mindfulness.

Anywhere Mindfulness

Decide randomly or with purpose somewhere in your day to tune into your environment.

At work, in the car, walking to the store; allow yourself to tune into your environment.

Take a deep belly breath and proceed for a time you allot, whatever duration, and soak in your present reality through your senses.Note without noting the smells, tastes, and touches of your life right now.In this practice, embrace external distractions, whether someone is waving to you, or you hold the door for someone, just allow it to be, moment to moment,

Chapter 11: Mental Disorders Associated With Ptsd

People with PTSD may have painful feelings of guilt about surviving a horrible event, when others didn't. They may also have feelings of guilt about what they had to do in order to survive. Phobic avoidance of activities or situations that resemble or represent the initial trauma may hinder social associations and result in divorce, marital conflict or inability to get or keep a job.

Signs and symptoms that are likely to occur, which are more likely to be caused by an interpersonal stressor (e.g. physical or childhood sexual abuse, being taken hostage, torture, domestic violence, incarceration like a prisoner of war or perhaps in a concentration camp are implicated in:

impulsive behavior

self-destructive behavior

somatic complaints

feelings of shame

hopelessness or permanent feeling of despair

inactivity

complete loss of belief in previously sustained values

social withdrawal

hostility

impaired relationships

feelings of constant threat

changes in the personal characteristics of the individual

There might be an elevated chance of Panic Attacks, OCD, Agoraphobia, Social Fear, Major Depression Symptoms, Substance-Related Disorders, Impulse

Control Disorders and Somatization Disorder.

Veterans

The rise of PTSD is documented by the increasing number of veterans recognized as victims of this terrible mental disorder. The following list of resources could be of some use if you are a veteran who has been experiencing any of the following

symptoms of PTSD (a wide variety of symptoms may be signs you are experiencing PTSD):

Feeling upset by things that remind you of what happened.

Having nightmares, vivid memories, or flashbacks of the event that make you feel like it's happening all over again.

Feeling emotionally cut off from others.

Feeling numb or losing interest in things you used to care about.

Becoming depressed.

Thinking that you are always in danger.

Feeling anxious, jittery, or irritated.

Experiencing a sense of panic that something bad is about to happen.

Having difficulty sleeping.

Having trouble keeping your mind on one thing

Having a hard time relating to and getting along with your spouse, family, or friends.

It's not just the symptoms of PTSD but also how you may react to them that can disrupt your life. You may:

Frequently avoid places or things that remind you of what happened.

Consistent drinking or use of drugs to numb your feelings

Consider harming yourself or others

Start working all the time to occupy your mind

Pull away from other people and become isolated

What is the Treatment for PTSD?

Two types of treatment have been shown to be effective for treating PTSD: ***counseling and medication***. Professional counseling can help you understand your thoughts and discover ways to cope with your feelings. Medications, called selective serotonin reuptake inhibitors, are used to help you feel less worried or sad.

In just a few months, these treatments can produce positive and meaningful changes in symptoms and quality of life. They can help you understand and change how you think about your trauma—and change how you react to stressful memories.

You may need to work with your doctor or counselor and try different types of treatment before finding the one that's best for dealing with your PTSD symptoms.

What Can I Do If I Think I Have PTSD?

In addition to getting treatment, you can adjust your lifestyle to help relieve PTSD symptoms. For example, talking with other Veterans who have experienced trauma can help you connect with and trust others, exercising can help reduce physical tension, and volunteering can help you reconnect with your community. You also can let your friends and family know when certain places or activities make you uncomfortable.

Your close friends and family may be the first to notice that you're having a tough time. Turn to them when you are ready to talk. It can be helpful to share what you're experiencing, and they may be able to provide support and help you find treatment that is right for you.

Take the Next Step - Make a Connection

Whether you just returned from a deployment or have been home for 40 years, it's never too late to get professional treatment or support for

PTSD. Receiving counseling or treatment as soon as possible can keep your symptoms from getting worse. Even Veterans who did not realize they had PTSD for many years have benefited from treatment that allows them to deal with their symptoms in new ways.

You can also consider connecting with:

Your family doctor: Ask if your doctor has experience treating Veterans or can refer you to someone who does

A mental health professional, such as a therapist

Your local VA Medical Center or Vet Center: VA specializes in the care and treatment of Veterans

A spiritual or religious advisor

"I thought I was being brave by ignoring it. But I was really being brave by facing up to it."

In addition, taking a self-assessment can help you find out if your feelings and behaviors may be related to PTSD. This short list of questions won't be able to tell you for sure whether or not you have PTSD, but it may indicate whether it's a good idea to see a professional for further assessment. If you believe you may be living with PTSD and are ready to take the next step, find a professional near you who may be able to help.

Chapter 12: Dealing With Category D Symptoms

Sufficient endurance conduct is a vital "endowment of nature." Humans have been genuinely effective in lessening the danger to life. All things considered, going across a road or driving a vehicle requires expanded readiness so as to endure. Cataclysmic events, for example, the ongoing tidal wave and man-made calamities, for example, war, fear monger assaults, slaughtering, looting, sexual and physical maltreatment, and plane accidents show how helpless we are. In the wake of enduring such an occasion, individuals need nuts and bolts—nourishment, cover, therapeutic consideration, and encouragement. These days mental consideration has been added to this rundown of fundamental requirements for certain individuals.

Specialists should know whether and when mental assistance is vital. The new rule on overseeing post-horrible pressure issue in essential and auxiliary consideration from the National Institute for Clinical Excellence (NICE) fantastically outlines the encounters of sufferers and carers and gives proof and exhortation on intercessions for grown-ups and children.1 The rule gives extraordinary thoughtfulness regarding "debacle arranging"; the requirements of ex-military staff, casualties of abusive behavior at home, and displaced people and refuge searchers; and the job of the non-statutory segment, underscoring the expansive effect of injury in present day society. Giving more regard for the nature and importance of post-awful pressure issue in a social and recorded setting would have made the rules total.

At the point when manifestations, for example, flashbacks, rest issues, trouble in concentrating, and passionate lability are gentle and have been available for under about a month after horrible mishaps, the rules suggest beginning attentive pausing. Behind this shrewd counsel lies the proof based end that early mental intercession, frequently called questioning, has no impact in anticipating post-horrendous stress issue; for sure, regardless of detailed high fulfillment, it may even be harmful.2-4 Clearly the standard practice of questioning after debacles and fiascoes should end. In any case, for dealing with the bedlam, material misfortunes, misery, and outrage—for instance, after a fear based oppressor assault—no indisputable proof is accessible yet on how a fiasco stricken network recovers control.

As per the NICE rule, treatment is essential when, in the outcome of injury, post-horrible pressure issue, misery, suicidality, compulsion, restoratively unexplained physical side effects, or dissociative issue emerge. The danger of creating post-horrendous pressure issue after injury is 8-

13% for men and 20-30% for women,5 with a year pervasiveness of 1.3% to 3.9%,6 making a colossal weight on society.

Post-horrendous pressure issue is essentially a deregulation of the dread framework. Dread is an essential feeling on occasion of peril, and is trailed by a stress reaction—battling, solidifying, or escaping. This endurance framework relies upon evaluating dangers so as to start endurance behaviour.7 Once the risk or injury is finished, the dread framework ordinarily quiets down following a couple of days or weeks. In post-awful pressure issue this framework neglects to reset to typical, keeping the sufferer hyperalert, filtering for hazardous signals as though the occasion may happen once more.

The turmoil is subsequently described by automatic, tireless recalling or remembering the awful accident in flashbacks, striking recollections, and intermittent dreams. The individual attempts to abstain from recalling the injury, by dodging its area or TV programs about it. Diligent manifestations of expanded excitement, for example, hypervigilance, overstated frighten reaction, dozing issues, peevishness, and trouble concentrating, are a piece of the turmoil. Comorbidities, for example, misery, substance misuse, and other nervousness issue are the standard instead of the exemption. Passionate desensitizing, for example, feeling isolates from others, is likewise observed—for instance in officers subsequent to peacekeeping missions.

The NICE rule deliberately audits the proof for both mental and pharmacological mediations. As first line treatment NICE suggests injury centered mental treatment. Both distributed and unpublished information demonstrate just constrained viability for few pharmacological intercessions, so NICE prescribes not utilizing drugs as first line treatment.

The best treatment for resetting the dread framework is psychological conduct therapy.8 By fanciful presentation to the horrendous accident the dread response will diminish in time. Ideas about the self that are provoked by the occasion, for example, feeling "frail," liable, or insusceptible, are supplanted by progressively sensible perceptions. The rule likewise underpins, yet not as unequivocally, treatment with eye development desensitization reprocessing, which uses a distractive move of respective incitement after presentation to diminish the passionate lability identified with the injury.

An unanswered inquiry remains whether the elevated feeling of dread in post-horrendous stress issue is identified with the occasion or to the concealment of bizarrely compelling feelings of despondency and animosity realized by the awful experience.9 Like Summerfield we accept that more consideration ought to be paid to the significance of shocking encounters, breaking the sufferer's perspectives about life,10 in spite of the fact that proof on this viewpoint is deficient. We additionally concur with the rule about focusing on the regular comorbidities of post-awful pressure issue, (for example, misery and uneasiness), however the proof is still very limited.1

Regardless of the presence of powerful psychosocial medications, 33% of patients won't recuperate fully.11 Comorbidity, chronicity, and the aggregation of intense and ceaseless pressure may disclose the restricted reaction to treatment. Additionally, from a developmental perspective one can perceive how "the endowment of nature" of recollecting and gaining from peril may confine what is achievable in treating post-horrendous pressure disorder.12 We can't erase the memory of injury.

Chapter 13: The Four F's: Fight, Flight, Freeze And Fawn

A more complete and accurate description of this instinct is the fight/flight/freeze/fawn response. The complex nervous system wiring of this response allows a person in danger to react in four different ways.

A fight response is triggered when a person suddenly responds aggressively to something threatening. A flight response is triggered when a person responds to a perceived threat by fleeing, or symbolically, by launching into hyperactivity. A freeze response is triggered when a person, realizing resistance is futile, gives up, numbs out into dissociation and/or collapses as if accepting the inevitability of being hurt. A fawn response is triggered when a person responds to threat by trying to be pleasing or helpful in order to appease and forestall an attacker. This fourfold response potential will heretofore be referred to as the 4Fs.

Traumatized children often over-gravitate to one of these response patterns to survive, and as time passes these four modes become elaborated into entrenched defensive structures that are similar to narcissistic [fight], obsessive/compulsive [flight], dissociative [freeze] or codependent [fawn] defenses.

These structures help children survive their horrific childhoods, but leave them very limited and narrow in how they respond to life. Even worse, they remain locked in these patterns in adulthood when they no longer need to rely so heavily on one primary response pattern.

It is important to understand that variances in the childhood abuse/neglect patterns, birth order, and genetic predispositions result in people polarizing to their particular 4F type.

In the next section we will explore examples of how children are driven into these defenses by traumatizing parents. The four children in the vignette below match the four basic types of trauma survivors:

Bob=Fight - Narcissistic

Carol=Flight - Obsessive/Compulsive

Maude=Freeze - Dissociative

Sean=Fawn - Codependent

More About Trauma

Trauma occurs when attack or abandonment triggers a fight/flight response so intensely that the person cannot turn it off once the threat is over. He becomes stuck in an adrenalized state. His sympathetic nervous system is locked "on" and he cannot toggle into the relaxation function of the parasympathetic nervous system.

One common instance of this occurs when a child is attacked and hurt by a bully after school. He may remain in a hypervigilant, fearful state until someone takes action to insure him that he will not be revictimized, and until someone helps him release the hyperactivation in his nervous system.

If the child has learned through experience that he can come to at least one of his parents when he is hurting, frightened or needing help, he will tell mom or dad about it. With them, he will grieve the temporary death of his sense of safety in the world by verbally ventilating, crying and angering about it.

Moreover, his parent will report the bully and take steps to assure that it will not happen again, and the child will typically be released from the trauma. He will naturally relax back into the safety of parasympathetic nervous system functioning.

"Simple", one incident traumas can often be resolved relatively easily if Cptsd is not already present.

If however the bullying happens on numerous occasions and the child does not seek help, or if the child lives in an environment so dangerous that the parent is powerless to ensure a modicum of safety, it may take more than parental comforting to release the trauma. If the trauma is not too continuous over too long a time, a short course of therapy may be all that is needed to resolve the trauma, provided of course the danger in the environment can effectively be remediated.

When the trauma however is repetitive and ongoing and no help is available, the child may become so frozen in trauma that the symptoms of "simple" ptsd begin to set in. This can also occur during the prolonged trauma of combat or entrapment in a cult or domestic violence situation.

If however, a person is also afflicted by ongoing family abuse or profound emotional abandonment, the trauma will manifest as a particularly severe emotional flashback because he already has Cptsd. This is particularly true when his parent is also a bully.

Chapter 14: Support

Having a strong support system and also learning how you can make things better for yourself with a positive attitude and equally positive thought s and actions will lead you to the end of the treatment road in no time. Follow these simple tips on things you can do to make the whole process better for you and for those who support you.

Stick to the plan. Feeling a change within yourself from the therapy and medication won't happen immediately, it has been said that some medication takes up to 2 weeks before effects begin to be felt. Be patient and know that the professionals helping you as well as your family are there to cheer you on.

Improve your knowledge on PTSD – the more you know about your condition the better and quicker your treatment will be. By conducting research on the different methods used to deal with PTSD you find out the goal to these and form a set path for yourself. By knowing about the different medication involved, you give yourself awareness on what to expect.

Make sure you get enough sleep. Eat healthy, exercise if you can. And avoid nicotine, alcohol and caffeine which have been proven to intensify anxiety.

Never self-medicate – remember that medication is different and customized in dosage and frequency depending on each unique individual. Just because someone has the same disorder as you do, doesn't mean that all you have to do is copy their dosage. Self-medicating can be dangerous and doesn't even promise the relief of PTSD symptoms.

Find distractions and decide on what you can do when you begin to feel anxious or afraid because you know that a uncontrollable and unstoppable thought is about to get into your head. Go for a jog, take a warm bath, or anything that could direct your mind towards something else.

Have a go-to person that you can come to with your problems, feelings and the development of your treatment. A support system is important but this 'top supporter' is equally as irreplaceable.

Sign up to a support group. There are lots of support groups out there, some of them even specifically for PTSD war veterans. Being in a support group and around people who know and understand your situation because they have been there themselves can offer you solace in knowing that you are not alone in this endeavor.

Supporting Someone with PTSD:

Supporting someone you know with PTSD can be just as important as them supporting themselves with all the right steps and actions that they can do. Support is an invaluable source to have when going through treatment for any mental illness and anxiety related disorder.

Improve your knowledge on PTSD. This will give you some insight on what your loved one is going through and help you to better understand why they act the way they do.

Don't let withdrawal be a setback. Support can sometimes also be hard to give, especially when someone is going through something difficult, you might often get pushed away. Don't let this stop you, even if you get pushed away, let that person know that though you understand that they need space, you will still always be there when you are needed. Alternatively, know to recognize when being pushed away is actually a sign that they need you or want you to be around.

Tell them that you can go to appointments if they want. Appointments can be difficult for people with PTSD as it is during these appointments that the very thing that fear and try to avoid gets faced head on. Make the offer to accompany them to appointments even if you just sit in the waiting room.

Listen. A person going through anxiety disorder will often be withdrawn and not prone to social interaction. If they talk, you listen.

Provide encouragement and applaud progress. Be the cheerleader for their treatment process.

Don't forget your own health. Be a good example and eat healthy, het enough sleep and exercise!

Remember that you have feelings too. If you find it difficult to cope with your loved one having PTSD, know that there are support systems for you as well.

Stay safe and avoid situations and places that you deem unsafe or where you think any more traumatic events might take place.

Chapter 15: Manage Your Time

Is your concept of time management simply "doing more in less time" or "finding extra hour in the day "?

Managing your time is more than just finding a way to do more in less time ... and we can not help knowing that there will be always only 24 hours in a day.

Managing your time is to actively use your imagination to:

1. spend time doing activities that make sense of your life;

2. organize your time so that you get the most out of the 24 hours you have in a day;

3. become aware of the real influence you have on your schedule over the course of a day

Some of the problems associated with poor time management are:

- always being in a hurry
- feeling worried, tense, anxious
- being late often
- decreased performance, lack of energy or motivation
- a sense of frustration
- a sense of impatience
- difficulty in setting and achieving goals

Do any of these signs apply to you? If yes, try the following suggestions:

Step 1: Take an inventory of your schedule

Step 2: Determine what you want to spend your time.

Step 3: Make sure your schedule reflects your values (see step 2).

Step 4: Become better organized.

Step 1: Determine what your values are

What do you want to spend your time on? What is important to you? What activities should you do conduct or wish to lead, and that are likely to contribute significantly to your work, your family, your relationships interpersonal or your personal growth?

Think about the 10 values that are most dear to you, and write them below. Think about what you see in your eyes value or meaning that may justify your time.

What are your values?

Below are some suggestions that may lead you to think about what may be important to you. Check out the following list and see if these values inspire you or help you determine your own aspirations or priorities.

Success or career advancement

The adventure

Full control of my workload

Courtesy and politeness

Creativity

A workplace respectful of people and their opinions

A suitable remuneration

Environmental concerns

Professional equality

Fame

The flexibility of my working conditions

Freedom of speech

Pleasure

Good customer relations

A good reputation

The health

The improvement of society

High standards of quality

integrity

innovation

Preserving my job

Respect for my promises

Posterity

Maintaining my dignity

My personal and professional development

The profitability

The respect

Security

God's service

Service to others

Step 2: Plan your schedule so that it better reflects your values

When you know what you are spending, you can look at these activities in terms of your values and priorities.

(defined in step 1). This will help you decide what changes you could, or should, make. In the light of observations that you have recorded in your agenda and values that you consider important, ask yourself the following questions and note your observations below.

- What activities in my agenda reflect my values and priorities?

- Which ones do not reflect them?

- Are there values that I neglect?

Then ask yourself the following questions and write down your answers below.

- What can I change about myself or what can I do to change my daily schedule so that this one

better reflect my values?

- What activities could I give up to focus on other things?

Step 3: Organize your time

Finally, think about what you can do to better organize your time and write your ideas below.

Organize your time: some tips

• Learn to set boundaries and say "no" as needed.

• Minimize the factors causing wasted time. Reduce the time you spend in front of the television, avoid to take your voicemail or e-mails at any time, flee unproductive meetings or activities which are conducted without a clear purpose and do not set you too ambitious goals.

• Use your time more efficiently. Do "two birds with one stone": write your "to-do lists" in queuing, watch TV doing housework, adapt your current activities to your energy level (eg, reserve difficult tasks for the times when you have the most energy, and work routines for periods when your energy level is the lowest).

• Get a diary and learn how to use it.

• Do not waste your time choosing between decisions with similar consequences. Play flip-flop, and get to work

- Set daily goals and plan long-term projects. Update your schedule regularly.

- Plan your phone calls more efficiently. If your contact is not available, try to find

the best time to reach him or leave him your number and let him know when he can you remember. Do not wait too long; do you hear in advance with your interlocutor on the length of your wait, or leave him a message.

- Assert yourself when faced with an interruption. Keep others informed of your constraints

of time. Politely say, "I only have a few minutes for this discussion. Or meet your colleagues in their office, so that you can leave the premises yourself when you want.

- Take a break when it becomes impossible for you to work effectively.

- Protect yourself against interruptions. Inform others of when you are available and for how many times, and times when you are not. Remain firm as to the respect of these periods.

• Do not put off work that you do not like. The longer you wait, the more difficult these tasks will be to carry out and the more stress you will experience until they are completed.

Conclusion

One of the most critical public health issues in modern medicine and psychology is the psychological response to traumatic stress. In the development of not only PTSD but also many, if not all other mental and somatic disorders, traumatic, stressful events and how individuals and groups deal mit them play a critical role. PTSD is a medical disorder that is extremely distressing and debilitating. It seems unlikely that any single perspective will be enough to provide a fundamental understanding and treatment of this disorder, PTSD comprised several complex multidimensional domains. PTSD Future research should bring new science and psychopathological paradigms with modern and refined diagnostic phenotypes. This paper proposes a model of seven perspectives for PTSD, loosely described in terms of complementary, overlapping, yet separate, phrases and concepts. The model integrates various aspects and treatment methods from psych pharmacotherapy to well-being therapy, to decrease disease and increase well-being through trauma and PTSD.

Our understanding of traumatic stress conditions has increased significantly since the diagnosis of PTSD was introduced 40 years ago. However, our potential for recovery from PTSD seems to have stalled in the last couple of decades, given this increasing awareness. While our therapy is relatively active, too many patients are not optimally able to respond, and many others cannot access it.

These issues continue to be a significant challenge in the field. Because millions of people affected directly by trauma, the limited success in providing efficient treatments for the majority of them leads to a significant burden on public health. In future years, it will continue to be a top priority to identify novel mechanisms that can be used to improve the outcome of treatment and overcome the main barriers to treating most healthcare systems on an evidence-based basis.

www.ingramcontent.com/pod-product-compliance
Lightning Source LLC
LaVergne TN
LVHW011950070526
838202LV00054B/4871